* * * * * * * *

Watch Your
F*cking Language

*

Also by Sterling Johnson

*

English as a Second F*cking Language

Watch Your F*cking Language

✳

How to Swear Effectively,
Explained in Explicit Detail and
Enhanced by Numerous Examples
Taken from Everyday Life

Sterling Johnson

(and a Distinguished Panel of Experts)

THOMAS DUNNE BOOKS
St. Martin's Griffin
New York

THOMAS DUNNE BOOKS.
An imprint of St. Martin's Press.

WATCH YOUR F*CKING LANGUAGE. Copyright © 2004 by Sterling Johnson. All rights reserved. Printed in the United States of America. For information, address St. Martin's Press, 175 Fifth Avenue, New York, N. Y. 10010.

www.stmartins.com

LIBRARY OF CONGRESS CATALOGING-IN-PUBLICATION DATA

Johnson, Sterling, 1939–
    Watch your f*cking language : how to swear effectively, explained in explicit detail and enhanced by numerous examples taken from everyday life / Sterling Johnson.—1st ed.
      p. cm.
  ISBN 0-312-31871-5
  EAN 978-0312-31871-0
    1. English language—Obscene words. 2. English language—Slang. 3. Swearing. I. Title: Watch your f*cking language. II. Title.

PE3724.O3J64 2004
427'.0—dc22

                        2004049746

For Notorious BGW

* * * * * * * * * * * *

Watch Your
F*cking Language

*

Introduction

✳

People will fuck.
—Kurt Vonnegut

People will also *talk* about **fucking.**

And if they want to communicate effectively, they won't say, "I made love many times last night." They'll say, "Last night **I fucked my brains out.**"

They won't say, "I have to see a man about a horse." They'll say, "I have to **piss** so bad my teeth are floating."

They won't say, "Oops! I broke wind." They'll say, "Wow! What a **fart!**"

When real people talk about real things, they use real language.

After *English as a Second F*cking Language* sold millions of copies worldwide, reports from readers both shocked and gratified me. I was shocked that some readers whose *first* language was English had not understood the nuances of swearing. I was gratified that they—like those for whom English is a *second* language—had benefitted from our work.

1

As we said in *English as a Second F*cking Language,* we swear in order to communicate. With that book we laid the groundwork for effective swearing. With this book we move to the next level.

Advanced language requires an understanding of colloquialisms and cultural idioms. You'll find an ample supply of them here. Many of these useful expressions won't sit well with the self-appointed forces of decency. They don't want us to read, hear, write, or say words that involve blasphemy, sexuality, or the natural parts and functions of our bodies.

And why is that? Because they're a bunch of **goddamned fucking assholes!**

Readers around the world have shared the joys that come from swearing. Many of you now serve as Honorary Members of My Distinguished Panel of Experts. Along with your suggestions and contributions—some of them to be found in this book—you let us know what you think of the forces of decency (the **goddamned fucking assholes** mentioned above).

You responded as individuals, yet you spoke to those forces in a powerful, unified voice. Your message was clear: **Fuck you and the horse you rode in on!** (See the **Idioms** section.)

If they refuse to listen to the voices of reason, that's their problem. We can only add: Stand aside, **assholes!** Make way for the *real* English language!

NOTE: Because we believe this volume will be a valuable resource for discussion groups, a **Discussion Point** has been included. Also a **Safety Tip.**

* * * * * * * * * * * * *

Short Stuff

*

If we piss as we walk, must we next shit as we run?
—MONTAIGNE (UPON OBSERVING A MAN WHO PISSED AS HE
STROLLED THE CHAMPS ÉLYSÉES.)

Acronyms, abbreviations, and initialisms are among the more annoying time-saving inventions. Still, time is money, and we might as well profit from the truncated swears so common today.

An acronym is a *pronounceable* word formed from the first letter or letters of a phrase. For example, the **ZIP** of the postal code stands for **Z**oning **I**mprovement **P**lan.

FUBAR

Fucked up beyond all recognition. Pronounceable, thus an acronym.

RTFM

You'd usually write this out. If you speak it, pronounce each letter. Try to pronounce it as a word and you're begging for a Heimlich maneuver. It stands for **read the fucking manual,** sound advice for men who

3

don't know what to do when their computers **fuck up** and the office nerd is **J.O.ing** (see below) in the supply closet.

BS

This stands for **bullshit** and is both noun and verb. Pronounce the letters "bee-ess."

SOL

This stands for **shit out of luck,** which means totally unlucky. It looks like an acronym but it isn't. It's an initialism. Pronounce the letters "ess-oh-el."

SOB

This stands for **son of a bitch.** Pronounce the letters "ess-oh-bee."

example:

Velma: I asked for a raise and the boss told me I was SOL. The company isn't making any money.

Elmer: The SOB was BSing you.

FY

For years **FYI** has meant **for your information.** Only with the advent of e-mail has **FY** enjoyed popularity as a stand-in for **fuck you.** Consider this e-mail exchange between a boss and an underling.

example:

Dithers: *To Bumstead:* FYI, In the interest of safety and economy, coffee breaks will be limited to three minutes, once a week.

Bumstead: To Dithers: FYI, FY!

DF

Pronounced: "dee-ef," this stands for **dog fucker** and is generally used metaphorically. Its uses are many. For instance, when addressing some **arrogant prick** with multiple academic degrees, you needn't acknowledge them all. Simply use **DF.**

example:

William: What's that DF on your sombrero stand for?

Jay: *Distrito Federal,* my good man. It's Mexico's capital city, home of the *Universidad Nacional Autónoma de México* where I earned three advanced degrees in Communication Arts.

William: Well, Professor DF, this is Boulder, Colorado, and here it means dog fucker.

On occasion, the **DF** in question may be an *actual* **fucker** of dogs.

example:

Byron: Did you hear that Chauncey Whitlock entered his Doberman at the Pebble Beach Dog Show last week?

Shelley: No. How did the old DF make out?

Byron: He got off easy: six months house arrest, two years probation, and a three-day suspension from the Del Monte Kennel Club.

CYA

Cover your ass. This is the motto of bureaucrats everywhere. It means that no matter what goes wrong, make sure you're not held responsible. Each letter is pronounced: "cee-wye-a."

example:
> *George:* Uh-oh. I accidentally launched a nuclear strike on Canada. What should I do now?
>
> *Karl:* CYA. Blame it on the media.

WAG

This is an acronym for **wild ass guess.** Making a **WAG** is the very essence of creative brain-storming, and also of coming up with dumb answers. Engineers tend to make **SWAGs, scientific wild ass guesses.** Although "wild" can mean extraordinary, as used here it means reckless, visionary, or unlikely. The **ass** is an intensifier, as in a "**big-ass** truck." (See **About the Size of It** section)

example:
> *Joe:* See that blonde with the wild ass? On the way back from the men's room I propositioned her. What do you think my chances are?
>
> *Jim:* The big-ass bouncer she was talking with is headed this way. My SWAG is he's going to kick your ass.

BFD

Pronounced "bee-ef-dee," it means **big fucking deal** and should only be used in e-mail correspondence.

McFuck

From the world of no-frills fast food we get the name for a **no-frills fast fuck,** also called a **quickie.**

In Great Britain, where the **McFuck** is done standing up, it's called a **knee trembler.**

In the United States the position is shunned by Southern Baptists, because it could lead to dancing.

P.O. 'd

Short for **pissed off,** meaning angered. Each letter is pronounced "pee-oh'd." But why bother? This initialism is both unnecessary and confusing.

example:

Arlo: I'm P.O.'d at the Post Office. I didn't get any mail.

Harlow: I got a ton of junk mail. I'm pissed off at the P.O. too.

Piss off!

When you anger someone, you **piss off** that person; however, the command **Piss off!** is British usage and means go away, get lost.

example:

Oscar: Would it piss you off if I put my hand on your thigh?

Jeeves: Piss off!

FAQ

This is pronounced "fak" and is not a swear. It is Internet shorthand for a **F**requently **A**sked **Q**uestion. Do not confuse it with tricky variations of **fuck,** such as **fug,** which Norman Mailer used in his 1948 novel *The Naked and the Dead.* He fooled no one. More than a half-century later, neither will you. As a former First Lady observed, "Just say **fuck!**"

MOFO

You'd think this corrupted shortening of **mother fucker** would be **MOFU,** but it isn't. It's a jovial term, usually used between friends.

example:

    Moe: Do you do karate, McArty?
    McArty: No, MOFO, kung-fu.

SNAFU

The acronym means **situation normal: all fucked up.** It is occasionally rendered as **situation normal: all fouled up.** This is witless and wrong. The descriptive phrase is also used as a noun.

example:

    Ed: I hear Bruce fouled up.
    Fred: Yeah. He's in jail for screwing chickens.
    Ed: Fowled up again. A typical Bruce SNAFU.

SMA

Not an acronym, it stands for **suck my ass.** When spoken, each letter is pronounced: "ess-em-a." It is occasionally used as a postscript to a letter. It has greater impact than **kiss my ass,** but the meaning is essentially the same.

example:

Miss Fitzgibbons:	See me after class, young man! We need to talk about your inappropriate language!
Bradley:	SMA! I don't talk to anybody without my lawyer present.

CF

This is a military term and—following the military fashion of making things more complicated than necessary—it is pronounced "**Charley Foxtrot.**"* The initials refer to a **cluster fuck,** which is an aggravated **SNAFU.**

example:

Commander Cody:	Sorry about wiping out your platoon with friendly fire. Must have given the wrong coordinates.
Corporal Payne:	No sweat, sir. I always expect a Charley Foxtrot from you, you fox-trotting ass-wipe.

MF

Mother fucker, clear and simple. Best written, although acceptable when spoken "em-ef."

---

*Charley stand for *C* and Foxtrot stands for *F* in the phonetic alphabet used by radio operators in the United States military. The fox trot, by the way, was a popular dance in the 1940s and is relevant to most army recruits over the age of eighty-four.

J.O.

Pronounced "jay-oh," this stands for **jerk off,** the verb. As a noun, a **jerk-off** is a useless sort of person. The noun form should not be abbreviated.

example:

> *Tom:* Can you believe it? Joe's watching a J. Lo video and J.O.ing in the hot tub.
>
> *Viv:* What a jerk-off!

The F-word

This is a poor substitute for **fuck.** For instance, it's jarring to the ears to hear, "Who the **F-word** knows?"

A

1. This means **ass,** but it is best used in compounds. Occasionally one hears, "He's a pain in the **A.**" This is foolish. Say **pain in the ass.**
2. In the expression **fucking-A, A** doesn't mean **ass.** It is an affirmation, perhaps related to the word "aye" used by sailors, or perhaps related to the letter **A** used in **A-1,** indicating something of first-quality.

example:

> *Ahab:* Hast thou seen the white whale?
>
> *Queequeg:* Aye, Captain. If you mean that big fat A-hole Ishmael, I fucking-A have!

A-hole

A barely acceptable abbreviation for **asshole.**

example:

> *Marge:* I got a D on my geography midterm, be-
> cause I thought the English Channel was the
> BBC. The teachers here are fucking A-holes.
>
> *Jim:* Fucking-A. On my electronics midterm I
> said AM radios don't work in the PM and the
> fucking MF gave me a fucking F.

BJ

Pronounced "bee-jay" it stands for **blow job.** Appropriate in spoken or written form.

MFWIC

Pronounced **mifwick,** this is sort of an acronym. It
is used at IBM and other high-tech companies and
means **mother fucker what's in charge.** (Note: it is
"what's," not "who's.") A **MFWIC** is a person who actually runs the show, not a figurehead.

example:

> *Ray:* I need an approval on this contract, is the
> CEO in?
>
> *Al:* Yeah—in his secretary. I'll handle it. I'm the
> MFWIC.

On occasion you may see **ESFL** (*English as a Second F*cking Language*) and **WYFL** (*Watch Your
F*cking Language*). **ESFL** is simply a grouping of initial letters, impossible to pronounce as a single word
by anyone not fluent in the Basque tongue. **WYFL** is
an acronym, and should be pronounced "wiffle."

We recommend you use the full titles.

Need to Know

ESFL
WYFL

Nice to Know

A
BJ
BS
CF
CYA
FAQ
FUBAR
J.O.
MOFO
RTFM
SMA
SNAFU
SOB
SOL
SWAG
WAG

Forget It

A-hole
BFD
The F-word
P.O.'d

Fucking-F

*

The term **F-word** is displeasing. It suggests that for **fuck** you should say **eff.** Rubbish! Eff lacks the satisfying hard "ck" sound of **fuck.** It and its derivatives should only be used in a pinch.

example:

During a codfish drought in Boston, a restaurant owner grew weary of telling a lady that the fish wasn't available. Finally he put a picture of a codfish in his window and wrote "COFD" across it. On her next visit the problem was resolved.

Doris: There's no "F" in cod.

Sam: You finally get it!

Banned Devices

❋

The shades of night were falling fast,
As through an Alpine village passed
A youth, who bore, 'mid snow and ice,
A stranger with a banned device,
Excelsior!
—HENRY WADSWORTH LONGFELLOW

Is the stranger's name "Excelsior" or is that the name of the **banned device?** The poet leaves it for us to decide. But if the device is a **dildo,** it may indeed be named Excelsior.* (And if the youth tries to take it into Alabama, he'll soon discover it's banned.†)

dildo

Dildos are **artificial pricks.** Like tofu hotdogs, they are meat substitutes and considered by some consumers to be better than the real thing.

---

*There is a hallowed tradition of naming **dildos.** In his novel *Naked Lunch,* William S. Burroughs, Jr., mentions three generations of dildos named "Steely Dan from Yokohama." The name "Excelsior" is appropriate for a dildo. It's Latin for **Ever Upward!** and appears on the official seal of New York State, one of the few states to choose a dildo as its motto.)

†Sex toys are banned in Alabama, one of many states to choose **dildos** as their lawmakers.

14

The basic dildo is simply a **dick-shaped object** that can be inserted into an orifice. Dildos range in sophistication from a simple candle to the high-tech Steely Dan III from Yokohama. (See footnote on previous page.) Cucumbers, carrots, and sundry legumes often fill the bill. (See **Vegetable** section.)

More advanced dildos are battery powered or plug into an electrical outlet (industrial strength dildos). They are called **vibrators** and are usually plastic or rubber, although silicone is the choice of power users.

strap-on

Strap-ons are **dildos** with special fasteners, such as straps, ropes, ribbons, Velcro, etc. They are worn by a second party, usually a friend.

Vac-U-Jac

For men, there are special devices for **jacking-off,** most notably, the **Vac-U-Jac,** an electrically powered **artificial pussy.** It comes with an attachment that plugs into a dashboard cigarette lighter.* When the Vac-U-Jac technology was combined with **Veg-a-Matic** technology, it led to hair-cutting devices such as the **Flowbee.**

example:

    Elroy: How come you're so pissed-off at your wife?

*****Safety Tip:** If you use your Vac-U-Jac during rush hour, be sure to buckle up.

Barry: She hooked up my Vac-U-Jac to the Veg-a-Matic and made her own Flowbee. When I got home last night she was giving hand jobs and haircuts to vegetarian sailors.

rubber

This is the most common term for a condom, even though not all are made from rubber. **Lambskins** are made from sheep intestines. In a pinch, some people have used **Saran Wrap.** Innovation has been common since the days of King Arthur's Round Table, as noted by Geoffrey Chaucer, Jr.

> *In days of old*
> *When knights were bold .*
> *And condoms weren't invented,*
> *They'd wrap their socks*
> *Around their cocks*
> *And fuck away contented.*

The devices are called **safes** in Boston, **East River eels** in New York City, **English caps** in Paris, and— dumbest of all—**French letters** in London.

the glove

Street term for a condom.

raincoat

Street term for a condom.

scumbag

Because ignorant people consider **jizz** undesirable, this was once a common term for a **rubber.** Later it came to mean a sluttish woman. Today it most often refers to a low-life, man or woman.

example:

> Leon: Damn it, I've got a hot date tonight and somebody stole all my scumbags.
> Jocko: Maybe it was that scumbag you were screwing on the corner table at Denny's last night.
> Leon: That was no scumbag, that was my wife— you scumbag!

French tickler

A condom gussied up with ribs, wings, nodules, feelers, tentacles or other such appendages. More a male fantasy than a tool for heightening milady's pleasure. Essentially it's a party hat for a **prick.**

ben wah balls

A legacy from ancient Japan, a **ben wah ball** is considered the lady's home companion. About the size of a golf ball, it is hollow and contains a smaller solid ball. Used in pairs, they wiggle and jiggle inside the **snatch** of the user, thereby causing orgasms, which is the whole point, right?

Need to Know

dildo
French tickler
rubber
scumbag

Nice to Know

ben wah balls
dipstick

Forget It

English cap
French letter

✳ ✳ ✳ ✳ ✳ ✳ ✳ ✳ ✳ ✳ ✳ ✳

Term Limits

✳

If you're afraid of going too far,
you won't go far enough.
—MICHAEL KINSLEY

In swearing, concerns of taste, tradition, and propriety
are ridiculous. There should be no limits to the terms
you use—and but one criterion: the words must enhance communication.

Far too often people complain that their minds are
imprisoned, even though they themselves built the
prisons.

example:
    Pat: I can't help myself. I have this overpowering
              desire to wear women's panties.
    Mike: Jesus, Patricia, it ain't that big a deal.

Even when we ourselves aren't hobbling our devel-
opment—spiritual and otherwise—those close to us
may try to do so.

example:

> *Brad:* The Bible talks about folks who "drink their own piss,* so why the big fuss when I brought it up the other night?
>
> *Janet:* Because we were at a wine-tasting, numb-nuts.

Well, fuck Janet and her secularism! If smarmy politicians can quote Scripture for their own purposes, so can Brad.

And so can you.

---

*2 Kings 18:27

Other Voices

Oh! Calcutta!
—1970s British play

Oh! Calcutta! is a pun on the French phrase *"O! quelle cul t'as,"* (Oh! what an **ass** you have!"). The revue, which introduced full-frontal nudity to the British stage, should have properly been titled *Tits, Balls, Cunts, and Pricks.* In the chauvinist atmosphere of the 1970s, author Kenneth Tynan barely escaped prosecution for preferring French to English.*

Today it's no crime to swear in a foreign tongue, but—with a few exceptions—it should be.

We're not against foreigners' swearing. Fuck no. We encourage people to swear in any language. However, the terms they use interest us only when they become part of our own tongue.

We've acquired many words directly from other languages: From the Spanish, *loco* (crazy); from the

---

*Despite his display of Francophilia, Tynan redeemed himself by being the first person to say **fuck** on British television.

Italian, *spaghetti* (spaghetti); from the German, *Rechtsschutzversicherung* (legal-costs insurance).

Most such words are useless—but not all.

Perhaps the only Spanish you know is **Chinga tu madre!*** (Fuck your mother!)

It may not make you the next ambassador to Mexico, but it's enough to get by on. You'll make your point. In fact, just saying, **Tu madre!** will do the trick.

We don't borrow words from other languages; we seize them, with no intention of giving them back. Often we improve on them, as with the German **fick** and the French **foutre.** Although they may have planted a seed, they are nowhere near as pleasing as our word **fuck.**

Need proof? Repeat each word aloud five times. You'll note that the German sounds like a hamster in heat and the French sounds like a Michelin tire going flat.

But the sound of **multiple fucks**—not to mention the satisfying mouth feel—is positively invigorating.

Certain foreign swears fit well into our language.

pendejo

Pronounced: *pen-DAY-ho,* the Spanish word for a pubic hair has a merry lilt to it. It's a useful alternate word for describing a person of no consequence; in other words, a dipshit or a jerk-off.

***Tu** is the familiar form of "your." In addressing a stranger or a senior citizen, the proper form would be **Chinga su madre!**

example:

> *Carlos:* Hey, señorita, your skirt is so short I can
> see a—
> *Maria:* Fuck you, *pendejo!* It's only a whisker
> from your girlfriend's moustache.

A note of caution: in its plural form the word may cause confusion.

example:

> *Ben:* Do you have panty hose under your Levis?
> *Jen:* Of course I have *pendejos* under my Levis.
> You think I am a baldy, you dipshit gringo
> jerk-off?

chingadero

Literally, "a man who fucks," but like the English term **fucker,** it's often used as the equivalent of a "whatchamacallit or a "thingamajig."

example:

> *Carlos:* Where the hell is that dang *chin-
> gadero?*
> *Don Juan:* If it was up your ass you'd know.
> *Carlos:* I'd have a perfect right to know.

Some foreign words are jarring to our ears, yet express concepts that demand our attention.

For example, in *For Whom the Bell Tolls,* Ernest Hemingway translates the Spanish expression *"¡Me cago en la leche de tu puta madre!"* as **I obscenity in the milk of thy whore of a mother.**

23

Why did Ernest substitute the vague noun "obscenity" for the sturdy verb **shit**? It's anyone's guess. Frankly, though, we doubt serious readers will waste time on such frivolous guessing games.

Too often, though, not only does the language itself come up short, the concept is outlandish. For instance, if you cut a fart at the Oktoberfest, a Bavarian might tell you, **Du hast einen Koffer stehen lassen.**

Translation: **You have left a suitcase standing.**

And people wonder why we have world wars!

In a heated discussion, we might tell someone, **"You're a son of a bitch."** Speakers of Croatian would likely say, **Jebo ti pas mater (A dog fucked your mother).**

example:

    Petrov: What are the two biggest lies a Croatian ever tells?

    Lazlo: You got me.

    Petrov: "The check is in your mouth" and "I promise not to come in your mailbox."

    Lazlo: Hilarious. By the way, a dog fucked your mother!

More useful is the Croatian term used when something is no big deal, or even nonexistent: **To je pickin dim.** Don't bother pronouncing it. Use the English translation: **cunt smoke.***

---

*Our Halifax correspondent informs us the Nova Scotian equivalent of **cunt smoke** is **fish nipples.**

    Dick: If we didn't find any weapons of mass de-
                  struction, what the fuck did we find?
    Donald: Cunt smoke.

Gaelic offers some excellent swears, but there's no sense learning the Erse tongue, since the Irish swear so well in English. Still, on St. Patrick's Day, Irish wannabees might enjoy getting **fucked up** on green beer and shouting **pogue mahone (kiss my ass!)** to other revelers.

Scheisse

Our panel debated including the German noun **Scheisse,** (pronounced "shy-suh") but decided against it, since it offers no advantages over the excellent English word **shit.** In fact, the extra syllable wastes valuable time.

example:

    Hans: I hope I don't step in any dog *Schei—*
    Orville: Look out!
    Hans: (staring at the sole of his shoe) *-sse!*
    Orville: Next time speak English—you dumb shit.

merde

Apropos of shit, the Italian **merda** and Spanish **mierda** are best left out of English conversations. The French variant **merde,** though, is acceptable for intellectual discussions.

example:

> *René:* I believe Sartre's existential view of life—as seen through the postmodern lens of Foucault—is truly epitomized by the artistry of your Jerry Lewis. Is it not?
>
> *Jackson:* *Merde!*

Fongool

This is an Italo-American adaptation of the Italian **Vai a fare in culo!** (Go to do it in your **ass!**) In the shorthand of southern Italy it's pronounced, **Va fa' en cul.** English has the excellent expression **Get butt-fucked!**—but occasionally the language of the immortal Dante is appropriate.

example:

> (Steve is dining at Ristorante d'Angelo in East Boston. He discovers his veal cutlet is cold in the center—a clue it's been frozen and then microwaved. He summons the owner.)

> *Angelo:* And how was the veal parmigiana, *signore?*
>
> *Steve:* Fongool!
>
> *Angelo:* (raising an eyebrow) I should get butt-fucked?
>
> *Steve:* With an ice-cold veal cutlet.

From Yiddish we get a number of useful swears.

schmuck

This word for a prick is now used by Jews and goyim alike to indicate a rotten person, a shithead.

26

putz

Another word for a prick, but not as intense as **schmuck.**

schlong

This is also a **prick,** but more literal. It comes from the Yiddish **schlang,** a snake.

example:

Miriam: You're not going to date that golfer schmuck, are you?

Becky: Maybe. He told me he's acclaimed for his long schlong.

Miriam: Bullshit. He's famous for his short putz.

Need to Know

schmuck
chinga tu madre
cunt smoke

Nice to Know

schlong
fongool
putz
pogue mahone

Forget It

Obscenity
A dog fucked your mother.
You left a suitcase standing.*

---

*Germans!

Nice Talk

This section—like life itself—is nasty, brutish, and short.

But it is necessary.

It deals with **euphemisms:** the mealy-mouth words and expressions that cloud meaning. Often they are used by a man who wants to be daring—but doesn't dare to.

Such a man will say **doo-doo** for **shit.**

Basically, he's trying to talk nice about things that *he* thinks are *not* nice. It's a pointless practice, because, besides himself, no one **gives a shit** what he thinks.

Worse, it's a dangerous practice. It **fucks up** communication.

A man using euphemisms is said to **talk like a man with a paper asshole.** He is cautious, timid, and indecisive. A man who'd sooner implode than **fart** in church.

example:

> *Sy:*   I think that car salesman was full of horse-feathers.
>
> *Regis:* You talk like a man with a paper asshole. He was full of shit. If a little old lady owned that car, why'd she have a siren mounted on the roof?

Euphemisms aren't meant to communicate; they're meant to protect the speaker's ego from his id—or some such Freudian **bullshit.**

On the other hand, we have **cacophemisms,** strong words used in place of less-effective "proper" terms.

For instance, those little doughnut-shaped pieces of paper used to strengthen the holes in ring-binder paper are sometimes called "reinforcing labels."

The problem is, a "reinforcing label" sounds like something that reinforces stereotypes, such as **frog-eating surrender monkey** for a Frenchman, **panty-sniffing butt bunny** for an Englishman, or **sheep hoser** for a male resident of El Paso, Texas.

Those little circles should be called **paper assholes,** a term everyone understands.

Should we avoid all euphemisms?

Heavens to Betsy* no! They are useful on the rare occasions that something less than an honest, straight-from-the-shoulder swear is needed.

---

*Occasionally sophisticates will use especially dim-witted euphemisms in speech, such as **"H. E. double hockey sticks"** for **HELL.** They consider it ironic rather than moronic. (They are wrong.)

sumbitch

A variation of **son of a bitch.** Why waste a full-blown swear on something as insignificant as, say, a shoelace?

example:

Lou: This sumbitch just don't want to stay tied.

Sue: Then use Velcro, you dumb son of a bitch.

scrotum

This word for a man's **ball sack,** by virtue of its pleasant sound, should be a swear word. Unfortunately, the forces of decency have co-opted it. Still, it's acceptable to use it for whimsical purposes.*

Need to Know

paper asshole definition 1
paper asshole definition 2

Nice to Know

scrotum
sumbitch

---

*As every school boy knows, the shout of "Scrotum!" in study hall is bound to add levity to an otherwise tedious occasion.

Forget It

doo-doo
give a hoot
H. E. double hockey sticks
heavens to Betsy

Tough Love

"Why can't we all just get along?"
—RODNEY KING

NOTE: This section will be nastier, more brutish, and shorter than the previous one—and invaluable to the reader.

Thanks to the movie *Full Metal Jacket,* it's not necessary to attend boot camp to learn U.S. Marine Corps jargon. For those who skipped both boot camp and the movie, here's all you need to know:

rip off your head and shit down your neck

A person who threatens you with this sort of behavior is peeved, but not dangerous. He is hoping to appear "tough" by exaggerating.

skull fuck

A person who uses this threat is a dangerous psychotic. Run, don't walk, to the nearest exit.

example:

Sergeant Fury:	I'm going to rip off your head and shit down your neck!
Madame Butterfly:	I think not, you big pussycat, because my uncle—that big guy in the ninja outfit—is about to gouge out your eyeballs and skull fuck you!

Need to Know

all of the above

Beastly Affairs

Q: How do porcupines fuck?
A: Carefully.
—AMERICAN FOLK RIDDLE

None of our Distinguished Panelists has **fucked** a porcupine. Most have no desire to do so. Still, we recognize that people do **fuck** a variety of beasts, both wild and domestic—and our language is the richer for it.

Inter-species mingling is ingrained in our culture. Consider:

- *Mary Had a Little Lamb* ranks in the top ten of America's best loved poems.
- Most American cities with "petting zoos" for children also offer "heavy-petting zoos" for adults.
- English majors at Yale are required to take at least one course in **animal husbandry.**

Unlike some members of the "superior" human race, *all* animals love to **fuck.** Still, some have acquired a special renown in that area. We admire them for it, and rightfully so.

rabbit, fucks like a

When we wish to compliment a woman on her zest for life, we say she **fucks like a rabbit.**

mink, fucks like a

If she is especially avid, we say she **fucks like a mink,** a term often heard in the heyday of Hollywood moguls.

example:

Samuel: How's the new secretary working out?
Harry: Terrific. She types like a mink.

horny

This is the most common term for being sexually excited. It comes from an older term, getting **a horn on,** meaning getting a **hard-on.** It's now used for both men and women.

three-balled billy goat, horny as a

A normal, **two-balled** billy goat is a **horny** creature, by any standards. But when a man's **throbbing cock** is about to burst through his trousers, we say he's as horny as the mythical triple-threat.

donkey rigged

Well hung. We may also say **hung like a bull** or **hung like a horse.**

pussy

A common term for a **cunt.** Another beastly term, **beaver,** refers to a **furry cunt** as seen by an observer.

camel toe

Like **beaver,** this term reflects the viewpoint of a voyeur. It describes a **cunt** displayed in bas-relief through tight pants. A woman's **camel toe** is equivalent to a man's **basket.** Men often pad their baskets with such bric-a-brac as rolled-up winter socks, zucchinis,* and furled Sunday editions of the *New York Times.*

Such **falsie baskets** are intended to give the impression the bearer is **well-hung.** Although many women augment their **asses, tits,** and eyelashes by artificial means, few pack their panties to enhance the **camel-toe** effect.

In the Middle East women are sometimes referred to as **cunts,** an example both of male chauvinism and *synecdoche*—using a part (in this case, the hole) to signify the whole (in this case, the woman). In Syrian bazaars you might hear a conversation like the following:

> *Achmed:* Look at the camel toe on that cunt!
> *Abdul:* The hell with the woman! Look at the cunt on that camel!†

In the United States a woman displaying an attractive camel toe is said to be hung like a doughnut.

---

*See **Vegetable** section.
†There are few women on the desert and **camel fucking** is common among traders who use the humped beasts to transport their wares. The practice has given rise to the following riddle:

Q: Why are camels called ships of the desert?
A: Because they're filled with merchant semen.

example:

> *Dwight:* Look at the camel toe on that honey!
>
> *Vince:*　Wow! She's hung like a doughnut!
>
> *Dwight:* A walking Krispy Kreme!

Of all animals, sheep have achieved the greatest renown among interspecieists. Lamb-loving lore is both vast and ancient, some of it enshrined in the ancient folk riddles of Scotland.

example:

> *Tessy:*　Why do you Scotsmen wear kilts?
>
> *Angus:*　So the sound of our zippers won't scare the sheep.

Although there's nothing wrong with **shagging sheep,** communication problems can arise.

example:

> *Moncrief:* Why spend money on a date when there are barnyard animals to be had?
>
> *Jerome:*　You cheap fucker!
>
> *Moncrief:* Are you calling me a sheep fucker?
>
> *Jerome:*　No. You're a pig fucker—and a cheap one at that.

America's attraction to lanolin lovelies came to prominence thanks to President Theodore Roosevelt. Although a big-game hunter, not all the animals he "bagged" ended up on the floor—at least not as rugs.

Once while pursuing bighorn sheep in the Rocky

Mountains, he found himself in a romantic frame of mind. He turned for advice to Fernando, his faithful Basque guide.

> *Teddy:* By George! This altitude has made me horny. What's the pussy situation here-abouts?
>
> *Fernando:* Wooly.
>
> *Teddy:* Bully!

The English-speaking world is not alone in its zeal for mounting mutton. Consider these facts:

- When an Australian wants a piece of lamb, he heads for the pasture, not the dining room.
- In Romania, virgin wool is unheard of.
- In those parts of France where possession of sheep is a felony, more households have a **moot**—*mouton pneumatique* (inflatable sheep)—than have a television set.

Still, those whose native tongue is English take the lead in **sheep shanking.***

In the United States, thanks to our cowboy culture, sheep play second fiddle to cattle. America's love affair with the cowboy almost matches the cowboy's love affair with his cow. Before the days of portable radios,

---

*The **sheepshank,** a knot beloved of British sailors and felons, was originally used to secure sheep during the long, lonely voyage from England to Australia.

cowboys sang to their cattle and entertained one other with riddles, the most famous being:

Destry: What word best describes the ideal woman?
Hondo: Bossy.

cowpoke

This term needs no explanation. The clueless need only consider a much-loved American folk song:

> *Out on the prairie*
> *The cows start to prance*
> *Whenever a cowpoke*
> *Unbuttons his pants.*
> *With a tye-eye yippie-yippie-yay,*
> *etc.*

stump broke

This means domesticated. Breaking broncos occupies a small portion of a cowpoke's day. Far more time is spent training livestock to position themselves for a **poking.** A **stump-broke** cow, for instance, is trained to back up to the stump the amorous cowpoke stands upon.

example:
Caleb: Jed claims he used to be a stock broker.
Buck: *Livestock* broker, maybe. That stump-broke heifer he brought to the last roundup was sure a good investment.

boot broke

On dude ranches, a **boot-broke** goat is trained to drop its back legs into the novice wrangler's Tony Lama boots. This prevents premature separation and allows for mobility when it's time to hit the trail.

fuck ewe

Basque shepherds of Nevada, new to the English language, are often considered surly. Those traditionally hospitable folk get this bad rap from greeting English-speaking visitors with a cordial **Fuck ewe?**

beast with two backs, making the

Always on the lookout for innovative ways to mention **fucking,** Shakespeare spiced up *Othello* with this graphic image.

example:

> *Brabantio:* Daughter, have you and Othello been making the beast with two backs?
>
> *Desdemona:* I wish. This month's *Playboy* just came in, and the wanker's been down in the dungeon all day making the beast with one back.

asshole, skunk

People sometimes say, "I'm so hungry I could eat a horse." In actuality they would recoil in disgust from the Palomino Platter. The folks at Rosie's Roundup in Bozeman, Montana, know how to make their point clearly.

example:

> *Hopalong:* Rosie, I'm so hungry I could eat the ass-hole out of a skunk. What's the special today?
>
> *Rosie:* You're in luck.

asshole, darker than a woodchuck's

How dark was it? Lazy authors might settle for "dark as night." But not Stephen King, the **wicked fuckin' good*** scribe from Down East who presented this vivid image to an international readership.

example:

> *Josh:* Goddamn, Gus, it's darker than a wood-chuck's asshole in here.
>
> *Gus:* Ay-uh.

Need to Know

stump broke

Nice to Know

beast with two backs
boot broke
darker than a woodchuck's asshole
eat the asshole out of a skunk

---

*See **Idioms** section.

Forget It

fuck ewe

Pig Fucking

Former President Lyndon Johnson once offered a recipe for political success: "Accuse your opponent of **fucking** pigs. Then watch him deny it."

Without taking sides on the issue, we'll note that the practice has given us a superb term of contempt: **fuckpig.**

It's recognized by Brits and Yanks alike, a charming aid to reconciling two diverse cultures that often have difficulty sharing the same language.

example:

    Jake: Get yer mitts off my knee, you fuckpig!

    Algernon: I *say!*

Going to the Dogs

✳

Old Mother Hubbard
Went to the cupboard
To get her poor dog a bone.
When she bent over,
She looked so good to Rover,
She got bred instead.
—WELSH NURSERY RHYME.

Man has long admired the dog for its obedience, loyalty, and ability to lick its **balls.**

example:
    Mutt: That damn pit bull's been licking his balls all afternoon.
    Jeff: Wish I could do that.
    Mutt: Go right ahead. But you'd better pet him first.

cock hound
    This woman is an enthusiastic **fucker,** relentless, dogged. She pursues **cock** with the zeal of a hot-blooded beagle harrying a hare.

hose hound
    Also an avid **fucker, hose** being another name for a **cock.**

slam hound

A **slam hound** is another story. She's often found in the vicinity of bus terminals, truck stops, and all-night diners. Rarely a professional, but often a semi-pro.

example:

> *Rafael:* I heard you scored with that slam hound at the Greyhound station. What did it cost?
>
> *Alex:* Nothing. I don't pay for pussy.
>
> *Rafael:* She did it for love?
>
> *Alex:* Well, yeah. And a bus ticket to Clearlake.

chowder hound

A woman who **swallows*** after the successful conclusion of a **blow job.**

doggy style

This is **fucking** on hands and knees with the man behind the woman. Other common styles include the **missionary position,** which is **fucking** face to face, and **New Age Fucking,** which is abstinence.

Need to Know

doggy style
missionary position
slam hound

---

*See **Feathered Friends** section.

Nice to Know

chowder hound
cock hound
hose hound

Forget It

New Age Fucking

Feathered Friends

*If the owl can't adapt to the
superiority of humans, screw it.**
—RUSH LIMBAUGH, *THE WAY THINGS OUGHT TO BE*

Bestiality can be a touchy subject, as poet William Butler Yeats knew when he wrote *Leda and the Swan*. Had he published his original version—*Leda and the Shetland Pony*—he'd never have won a Nobel Prize. In fact, he'd have been lucky to get a 4-H award at the Sligo County Fair. Even though Yeats played it safe, the publication of *Leda* dealt the final blow to **birdfucking** poetry.†

Long before the critics ganged up on Yeats, bird fucking was considered inappropriate behavior, as suggested by a classic riddle.

---

*Check out your state's fish and game laws first.
†Gerard Manley Hopkins almost dealt the death blow earlier with such suggestive, feather-ruffling lines as: "My heart stirred for a bird."

example:

> *Aristotle:* Why did the pervert cross the road?
>
> *Epictetus:* Because his dick was stuck in the chicken.

Our panel recommends you avoid **bird fucking,** or at least **bird-fucking** poetry. Still, we feel birds have made significant contributions to our language.

flip the bird

The generic bird is honored in this phrase. When we **flip the bird** to someone, we make a gesture with our fist closed and our middle finger extended. The **one-finger salute** signifies **Fuck you!** We may also say **give the finger.**

eat the bird

The **bird** is a **prick,** and cannot stand alone. This phrase means **Blow me!**

eat the hairy canary

A flowery way of saying **eat the bird.**

goose

To poke or grope somebody's **ass.** Derived from the attack mode of geese. **Goosing** dates back to antiquity. Inscribed at the base of Cleopatra's Needle in New York City's Central Park is the ancient riddle that won Caesar's heart:

> *Cleopatra:* What's the difference between a snake and a goose?
>
> *Caesar:* Ya got me, kid.

48

Cleopatra: A snake is an asp in the grass.
Caesar:　　D'oh!

swallow

This does not refer to a bird, but to the act of swallowing **jizz** while giving a **blow job.** Sometimes called the **white swallow.***

leg of the duck

In his novel *Ulysses,* James Joyce includes a song that employs this term for a **prick.**

> *I gave it Molly*
> *Because she was jolly.*
> *The leg of the duck.*
> *The leg of the duck.*

To use the term even once is imbecility; to use it twice, sheer lunacy.

---

*The average ejaculation contains aboutonia, ascorbic acid, blood-group antigens, calcium, chlorine, cholesterol, choline, citric acid, creatine, deoxyribonucleic acid (DNA), fructose, glutathione, hyaluronidase, inositol, lactic acid, magnesium, nitrogen, phosphorus, potassium, purine, pyrimidine, pyruvic acid, sodium, sorbitol, spermidine, spermine, urea, uric acid, vitamin B^{12}, and zinc.

These ingredients are no worse than what you'd find in a can of no-cal soda. However, the average ejaculation contains fifteen calories. According to our panelist Capistrano† (not her real name), "They add up."

†We call her Capistrano because she welcomes swallows.

pecker

This term for a **prick** is confusing. Birds don't have **peckers;** they peck with their beaks. Oddly, we don't call our **peckers** beaks; that's what we call our noses. Historians recognize the problem, noting that the only meeting James Audubon ever had with the Birdman of Alcatraz was fraught with confusion.

example:

James: Why do you say birds are smarter than men?

Birdman: Because they can eat with their peckers.

James: (Smiles, flips him the bird.) Fuck you, lifer!

fuck a duck

This has nothing to do with a bird. It's an expression of amazement and an example of reduplicated words, like fuddy-duddy, hanky-panky, or **fucky-wucky.**

example:

Dennis: Can you see what that farmer is doing?

Lucille: Fuck a duck! He's fucking a chicken.

choking the chicken

A term for **jerking off.**

eggs

A man's **balls.** It is never used in the singular.

example:

    Waitress: How are your eggs?

    Lamar: Wouldn't *you* like to know.

    Waitress: Not really, but we're trained to be polite to the assholes we serve.

Need to Know

give the finger
give the bird
goose
flip off
flip the bird

Nice to Know

eggs
fuck a duck

Forget It

The leg of the duck.

Fishy Business

Man, I'd go underwater and fuck fish for that kind of money, you just tell me who's payin'.
—ANONYMOUS BIKER QUOTED IN
HUNTER THOMPSON'S *HELL'S ANGELS*

Since antiquity, men have been attracted by the pheromones that create "the scent of a woman." King Solomon compared the fragrance to saffron, myrrh, and other costly spices. Today the comparison most often made is to fish. When jazz great Fats Waller sang, "I want some seafood, mama," he wasn't craving frozen fish sticks*

---

*You shouldn't crave fish sticks, either. They are high in artery-clogging trans fats and even the mere mention of them can create problems.

example:
>   *Henri:* So, monsieur, has it pleased you, the meal?
>   *Bruce:* It was horrible. Where did your chef learn to cook fish sticks?
>   *Henri:* Fish sticks? *Zut alors!* I thought you ordered fish dicks!

tuna taco

This is a **cunt,** and an edible one at that.

oyster*

Here's another. It's soft, smooth, and moist, and the pearl within this oyster is the clitoris.†

example:

Louise: That jerk just asked if he could stroke my oyster.

Thelma: He's got a set of oysters!

Louise: He asks again, I'll have 'em on a half shell.

Rocky Mountain oysters

These are **calf balls** (or **sheep balls**), a gourmet treat along the Continental Divide. Except for a few kinky cowboys (or kinky shepherds), people remove them from the beasts before eating them.

pearl diving

This is the act of eating a **tuna taco.**

snapper

A **cunt,** but beware! It's not named for a fish, but for its seeming ability to seize and entrap **pricks.**

Pricks, too, are associated with marine life.

---

*In the plural this is a whole 'nother bag. Usually used in the expression a **set of oysters,** it a term for a man's **balls.** Metaphorically, it refers to courage or boldness.

†In keeping with the nautical tradition, the clitoris is sometimes called **the man in the boat.** Although standing up in a boat is undesirable, an erect **clit** is a positive good.

flounder, pound the

The tasty flat fish gives us this term for **whacking off.** As a term for a **prick, flounder** cannot stand alone.

haddock, whack the

The haddock—an equally tasty fish, and one that makes an excellent chowder—gives us another term for **whacking off.** It too never stands alone.

example:

    Isaac: Excuse me, Cliff, I didn't realizing you were pounding your flounder.

    Cliff: No harm done, Isaac. Care to whack your haddock?

    Isaac: While watching the fishing channel? Think I'll pass on that.

trouser trout

A charming but inaccurate term for a **prick.** Real pricks don't have dorsal fins or sharp little teeth.

eel

Another name for a prick. It's used primarily in the expression **peeling the eel;** i.e., **jerking off.**

example:

    Heloise: Can someone help me put this worm on the hook?

    Captain Bligh: You could ask Fletcher, our deck hand. He's a master baiter.

Heloise:	I know. He's aloft in the rigging peeling his eel.*

fish monger

A **pimp.** This term would only be used by a demented lexicographer.

scrod

This is a type of haddock—but it is a fish and nothing more. Referring to it in a sexual sense causes confusion. Consider a Boston matron on her way to the fish market:

example:

Mrs. Cabot:	Driver, take me to Haymarket Square. I want to get scrod.
Louie:	Whatever you say, lady.
Mrs. Cabot:	Is there a problem?
Louie:	Nah. I just never heard that word used in the future pluperfect.

eel skin

A name for a condom (see **Devices** section).

Need to Know

pearl diving
peel the eel

---

*This is an example of "frigging in the rigging." (See **Frig It** section.)

pound the flounder
tuna taco
whack the haddock

Nice to Know

eel skin
frig
frigging in the rigging
oyster
oysters
snapper

Forget It

fish monger
fish sticks
scrod

   Discussion Point: There are no slang terms for "milt," which is **fish jizz.**

Frig It

The ropes that control a ship's sails are collectively called "the rigging." **Frigging** comes from the Middle English *friggen*, to quiver. When you're making your **clit** or your **dick** quiver, you're **frigging** yourself. Although used as a euphemism for **fucking,** it's best restricted to **finger fucking** or **jerking off.** Like the term **jerking off,** it may also be used metaphorically to mean passing the time heedlessly.

example:

> *Wimpy:* Why ain't Popeye here for your anniversary party?
>
> *Olive:* He's down at the harbor, frigging in the rigging.
>
> *Wimpy:* You want I should go get him?
>
> *Olive:* No, he can go fuck himself. I'll stay home and frig myself.

Our panel recommends you avoid using **frig** for one basic reason: Although it means **jerk off,** it is used as a substitute for **fuck,** and **jerking off** is no substitute for **fucking.** Still, we won't ban it outright, if only because middle-school students take such pleasure in hearing their history teachers pronounce "frigate."

＊ ＊ ＊ ＊ ＊ ＊ ＊ ＊ ＊ ＊ ＊ ＊

Slithery Things

＊

I'm the kind of person would fuck a brush pile
if I thought they was a snake in it.
—THOMAS MCGUANE, *NINETY-TWO IN THE SHADE*

Our panel has adopted a neutral stance on **brush fucking,** but we actively urge caution in reptilian/human sex. The results can be disastrous, as the American poet and song writer Stephen Foster noted in his only exploration of the subject:

There once was a girl from Decatur,
Who was fucked by a bull alligator.
Nobody knew
The results of that screw,
Because after he fucked her, he ate her.

Foster's cautionary work has been an effective deterrent, at least in regard to crocodilians. Snakes are another story. Perhaps because of male chauvinism, the phallic creatures have crept into our vocabulary and found a home.

snake

A **prick.** Ever since Eve, snakes have been getting bad press. Nevertheless, this is not a negative term. It's simply a matter of shape.

snake fuck

A noun denoting a **quick fuck** with an unappealing person. It's done for sexual gratification only.

example:

> *Geraldine:* I heard you and your ex were at the club last night. Did you two get back together?
>
> *Maude:* Yeah, for a three-minute snake fuck.

snake fucker

Oddly, this is *not* a person who participates in a **snake fuck.** But it is a low person indeed, one who can be counted on to behave in a slimy fashion.

example:

> *Fenwick:* Do you think Fensterman's ready for a partnership in the firm?
>
> *Fendall:* He's a real snake fucker.
>
> *Fenwick:* I agree. Tell him he's in.

python

A **large dick.** A term employed by boastful chaps, and one that invites debunking.

example:

    Abel: Honey, how'd you like to party with my python.

    Mabel: I'll pass, thanks. Looks more like an inchworm to me.

snow snake

Military personnel en route to chilly climes—such as Pt. Barrow, Alaska, or McMurdo Station in Antarctica—are warned against this creature. Supposedly it can crawl up your **ass** and freeze you to death.

The snow snake may be fictional, but there are confirmed reports of **anal-oriented** serpents.

Case in point: One afternoon in the late nineteenth century, bickering poets Emily Dickinson and Walt Whitman—the James Carville and Mary Maitland of their day—picnicked near Walden Pond. When a garter snake slithered by, Dickinson began to wax poetic. Whitman—fearing she'd attempt another of her annoying off-rhymes—cut her short.

    Emily: I spied a narrow fellow in the grass-

    Walt: Why don't you stick that narrow fellow up your ass!

living snake

Those who've read Terry Southern's *Candy* will recognize this term for a **cunt**—an especially cozy one. Others will only gasp in awe at the range of man's imagination. The term is of literary interest only.

lizard

This is the **prick,** as used in the expressions **bleeding the lizard** and **milking the lizard.** The former means **pissing,** the latter **jerking off.** In days gone by, when **jerking off** was frowned upon in the U.S. Army, the latrines offered opportunities for forbidden handiwork.

example:

Sergeant Bilko: Okay, Private, drop the gun!

Private Ryan: Aw, Sarge, I was just bleeding my lizard.

Sergeant Bilko: Shake it more than three times soldier, you're not bleeding it, you're milking it.

dragon

Also the **prick.** Also restricted to **pissing.** It's used in the phrase **draining the dragon.**

example:

Wilbur: Excuse me, I've got to drain my dragon.

Eustace: The dragon is a mythical beast.

Wilbur: So's the snow snake. But if I don't bleed this monster lizard soon my eyes are going to turn yellow.

Need to Know

snake fuck
snake fucker

Nice to Know

bleeding the lizard
draining the dragon
living snake
milking the lizard

Forget It

python

Vegetable

Q. What's better than roses on your piano?
A. Tulips around your organ.
—AMERICAN FOLK RIDDLE

To the serious communicator, the vegetable kingdom offers as many pitfalls as useful expressions. Consider the pea and the **pee.**

The first is a round green thing eaten by vegans. The second is **piss.**

Some think it clever to use the initial letter of the word **piss** in place of the word itself. They err. It's tiresome and tends to confuse people.

In *Ulysses,* James Joyce* has Cissy Caffrey say, "My mother cooks carrots and peas in the same pot."

To the reader, this presents no problem. To the listener—particularly one who has just dined at the Caffrey's—it can be disturbing.

---

*Readers of the **Feathered Friends** section may recall that this same James Joyce referred to a **dick** as the **leg of the duck.** It may have cost him the Nobel Prize.

lily

This is a word for the **dick** and is used only in the flowery phrase for **pissing,** "I have to **shake the dew off my lily.**" According to one authority, it's a common term. Perhaps among the clinically insane!

example:

    Napoleon: I think I'll shake the dew off my lily.
    Josephine: Suit yourself, you fucking loony, I'm off to take a piss.

The message is clear: Don't get flowery. **Piss** and be done with it.

urine

The medical term urine—and a foolish term it is—is even more confusing than **pee.**

Consider the situation of Renaldo, a chap suffering from the **clap.**

example:

    Ramon: What's the problem, amigo?
    Renaldo: Urine trouble.
    Ramon: *I'm* in trouble? At least I don't scream when I piss.

For the sake of your health, void your **piss;** for the sake of clarity, avoid **urine.**

In terms of sexual matters, vegetables fall into two categories. Those that can be penetrated and those that can penetrate. In other words: those **you fuck** and those that **fuck you.**

Foremost among the first category is the melon. In Ernest Hemingway's *For Whom the Bell Tolls*, the salty Pilar observes, "The melon of Castile is for self-abuse."

Our panelists don't condone the term "self-abuse" (see **ESFL**), but they agree that a succulent melon that's been warming in the sun all afternoon can compare favorably with the **liver box** (see **ESFL** again) on those occasions when live companionship is hard to come by.

example:

> *Farron:* Damn you, Lafe. What were you doing all scrooched up in my melon patch?
>
> *Lafe:* I cut a plug out of a melon and then fucked it.
>
> *Farron:* That's disgusting, wasting a good melon.
>
> *Lafe:* Didn't waste it. When I was done I re-plugged it.

Tits are sometimes referred to as melons. This is inexact, since there is a vast size difference between cantaloupes and watermelon—just as there is between **titties** and **bazongas.** No reputable produce broker would ever consider ordering a truckload of **tit-size** melons.

Even gynecologists get caught up in melon-related confusion.

example:

> *Dr. Savvy:* I recently had a patient with a clitoris like a watermelon.

Dr. Kildare: That's huge!

Dr. Savvy: Not the size—the taste.

We advise staying away from melons. Catching glanders from your neighbor's mule is embarrassing; catching a plant disease is humiliating.

Thanks to Sigmund Freud and his concept of phallic symbols, the category of insertable vegetables came to the fore. (And aft—see **corn-hole,** below.)

Freud convinced patients who dreamt about cucumbers, carrots, zucchinis, and other elongated vegetables, that they were actually dreaming about **dicks.** Eventually he admitted he was just having a little joke (*ein klein Dickwitz*) at the expense of his gullible patients. "If you vant to dream about dicks," he confessed, "you vill dream about dicks!"

cabbage patch

This is a term for a **cunt.**

example:

Simeon: Have you seen that danged hired hand? I wanted him to work in my barn today.

Nate: Tough luck. Your wife wanted him to work in her cabbage patch.

corncobbing

This is an alternate term for **corn-holing.**

corn-holing

This is a term for **butt-fucking.**

cornhusking

If you've ever husked corn, you'll understand how it relates to **jerking-off,** and vice-versa.

example:

    Clem: What's taking you so long in there, boy?

    Chad: I'm husking corn, Dad.

    Clem: You keep doing that, you'll go blind.

    Chad: I know. I'm going to quit soon as I need glasses.

cucumber

This is a metaphorical term for a **hefty dick,** a **choad.** According to sociologists, the actual **cucumber** has overtaken the actual **carrot** as the most popular substitute for a **dick.** Many feminists prefer these **organic dildos** to the mechanical type, and almost all find them superior to men. There *are* dissenters.

example:

    Andrea: I'll never understand why the Goddess created men.

    Germaine: Because cucumbers don't take out the garbage.

potatoes

Most people will agree that the potato is **unfuck-able.** There have been reports of army cooks **fucking** mashed potatoes, but it's more likely they **fucked-*up*** the mashed potatoes.

falsie basket

Our panelist advise you to forget **fucking*** or **being fucked** by a potato. Still, you can use the humble tuber as a make-shift **cod piece** or **falsie basket.** More than one actor on *Baywatch* has augmented what nature gave him by stuffing a potato in his bathing trunks. '

Be forewarned! If you don't fully grasp the concept, the results can be disastrous.

example:

> *Zack:* I tried your potato idea and the girls just laughed at me.
>
> *Mitch:* Put it in the *front,* dipshit!

Need to Know

corn-holing
cornhusking

Nice to Know

cabbage patch
corncobbing
falsie basket

---

*When a former U.S. President said, "I don't like fucking broccoli," many media people didn't realize he used **fucking** as an intensifier. He didn't mean he didn't like to **fuck** crucifers; he meant he didn't like to *eat* them. (We *think* that's what he meant; history will be the final judge.)

Forget It

cucumber

melons

shake the dew off the lily

Strange Fruit

❋

Among those fruits which may be said to resemble sexual organs other than the **cock** and the **cunt,** we must reckon the kiwi.

The fruit of the Chinese gooseberry (*Actinidia chinensis*), the delicious kiwi has a fuzzy outer skin that gives it a striking resemblance to a green monkey's **testicle.**

Even highly trained scientists can mistake it for a toxic substance.

example:

Dr. Noh: What in hell are you eating, Kabuki? It looks like a green-monkey nut!

Dr. Kabuki: No, Noh. It's a hairy kiwi. Care to try one?

Dr. Noh: I'll pass. Sound like suicide to me.

Mineral

We go strolling through the park,
Goosing statues for a lark,
If Sherman's horse can take it, why can't you?
—AMERICAN FOLK SONG

Aside from the example of **statuary rape** cited above, the mineral kingdom does not loom large in the vocabulary of forbidden language.

inorganic sex
Don't use this term. There is *always* an **organ** involved.

p'r'aps-p'r'aps
This Cape Cod expression refers to **fucking** on the beach. It comes from the logical conjecture "Perhaps she'll get **sand in her ass,** perhaps she won't."

example:

Clarence: I was thinking of having a picnic over at the National Seashore. Get some sun, surf, and maybe play a little p'r'aps-p'r'aps. Interested?

Annabelle: No.

rocks, getting off

A man's **balls** are sometimes called **rocks,** and when he has an **orgasm** he is said to **get his rocks off.** A striking example of gender equality, this rollicking, rough-and-tumble phrase now also applies to women.

example:

    Jack: Talk about weird side effects! Every time Jill sneezes she gets her rocks off.

    Mack: What's she taking for it?

    Jack: Pepper.

Need to Know

rocks, getting off

Nice to Know

p'r'aps-p'r'aps

Forget It

inorganic sex

About the Size of It

There once was a lady named Prue,
Who said as the bishop withdrew,
"The vicar is quicker and slicker and thicker
And has two more inches than you."
—BENJAMIN HILL

Although Prue makes no value judgments, we doubt the bishop enjoyed the comparison. Despite the decrees of some **needle-dick** sexologists, **prick size** counts. The following dialogue demonstrates that.

example:

Hugh: Want to come up to my place? I'm dynamite in bed.

Shirley: I'll pass. I'm afraid of dynamite when it's only got a three-inch fuse.

The size of our body parts plays an important role in our language. We say a self-important person has a "big head." We say a generous person has a "big heart." These images, however don't interest us, our concern being **balls, dicks, cunts,** and **asses.**

big balls

We say that a spunky man has **big balls.** Since we can also say it of a woman, it's obviously metaphorical.

example:

    Ari: Jane called her boss a short-horn.

    Colin: Wow! She's got big balls!

Actual **big balls** are examined in a popular military song whose lyrics* have been attributed to Rudyard Kipling:

How Do They Hang?†

> *Do your balls hang low?*
>
> *Can you swing them to and fro?*
>
> *Can you tie them in a knot?*
>
> *Can you tie them in a bow?*
>
> *Can you throw them o'er your shoulder,*
>
> *Like a Continental soldier?*
>
> *Do your balls hang low?*

whopper

This is the most common term for a **large dick.** It is neither an expression of length nor girth, but of overall size.

---

*Musicologists say the melody is taken from "The Sailor's Hornpipe." Normal people know it as the tune from "They Don't Wear Pants on the Sunny Side of France."

†Basically, the song asks a single question. Kipling broke it into several sentences to avoid the confusion his rival Francis Scott Keyes caused with "The Star Spangled Banner," his own notorious one-sentence question.

example:
> *Herb:* Care to go to McDonald's for a Big Mac?
> *Amy:* I'd rather stay home and have a whopper.

chubby

This is a **fat dick.**

choad

This is fatter than a **chubby.** This **dick** is almost wider than it is long. It's a term favored by artist S. Clay Wilson, chronicler of gay pirate life.

example:
> *Captain Hook:* Say, matey, how's about I fondle your choad!
> *Captain Kidd:* My pleasure. But use the other hand, please.

beer can

This sort of **dick** has the proportions of a twelve-ounce can of Budweiser.

short horn

This is a person with a **small dick.** During the Roaring Twenties, a sign over the urinals in the Plaza Hotel men's room said: SHORT HORNS STEP UP CLOSE; THE NEXT MAN MAY BE BAREFOOT.

fucking the night

This is a way for a man to imply a woman's **pussy** is too large. (Or that his own **dick** is too small.)

example:

> Betty: Was it good for you?
>
> Arnold: It was like sticking my dick out a window and fucking the night.
>
> Betty: Have you ever considered screwing chipmunks?

elephant woman

This is a woman with an exceptionally **large pussy.** The term comes from the *Kama Sutra,* the classic sex manual of India. It's clearly a relative term, since the author's pen name *Vatsyayana* is Hindi for **peanut dick.** It's a useless term that we include only to offer the reader international flavor.

big-ass

This doesn't refer to a person's actual **ass.** This **ass** is simply an intensifier for "big."

lard ass

This is a term for a person with a **big ass.** It often implies the person is slovenly, lazy, or both.

example:

> Ernie: What a lard ass that Roger is!
>
> Bernie: Yeah, and the lazy pig's sure got a big-ass ass.

Need to Know

big-ass
big balls
choad
whopper

Nice to Know

beer can
chubby
fucking the night
lard ass

Forget It

elephant woman

Traps

*I had nothing to offer anybody
except my own confusion.*
—JACK KEROUAC, ON THE ROAD

On the road to effective communication there is much confusion. Beware!

assholed

In Australia, **getting assholed** means getting drunk. In Turkish prisons, Reading Gaol, and the steam baths of Castro Street it has a different meaning.

example:

Ellwood: How was you're little stay in the stony lonesome?

Jake: I got hassled but not assholed. My farts still whistle.*

---

*See **Idioms** section.

beaver cleaver

A beaver is a **cunt,** and that which cleaves it is a **prick.** Unfortunately, nostalgia buffs confuse the term with Beaver Cleaver, from the television show *Leave It to Beaver.* Even the show's writers got confused, as indicated by this exchange between Beaver's parents, June and Ward.

example:

> *June:* How's our little Beaver Cleaver today?
> *Ward:* It's as hard as Chinese arithmetic.(pouts) And it's not so little, darn it!

charity fuck

When a person **fucks** an unappealing person out of the goodness of his or her heart, it is a **charity fuck.** If the unappealing person is *grotesquely* unappealing, it is a **mercy fuck.** Although the good Samaritan tries to accomplish the fucking quickly, it is not a **McFuck.***

cunt struck

A **cunt-struck** man is always horny, always seeking what the philosopher Ludwig Wittgenstein called "the next piece of ass."

eye-opener

The first drink of the day. But also a tremendous **hard-on** that draws so much of a man's skin he can't shut his eyes.

---

*See **Short Stuff** section.

example:

    Patron: Barmaid, I need an eye-opener—a good stiff one!

    Barmaid: Ditto.

Honoré Balzac

In France, the author's name is venerated. In America it is usually confused with **ornery ball-sack,** one of the unintended consequence of screwing someone with gonorrhea.

example:

    Jacques: Are you familiar with Honoré Balzac?

    Larry: Fucking-A! I caught a wicked dose of clap on my last visit to the *Bibliotèque Nationale.*

horse cock

Horse cock has nothing to do with being **hung like a horse.** It is simply a Britishism for "nonsense."

example:

    Clyde: My prick's so big I have to fold it double to wear Bermuda shorts.

    Dale: Oh, horse cock!

    Clyde: Yeah.

pussy whipped

A **pussy-whipped** man is dominated by his wife; or—if he's polygamous—his wives.

example:

> *Curly:* How come Brigham ain't going to the cat
> house with the rest of the crew? I thought
> he liked to get laid?
>
> *Zane:* He's cunt struck, all right, but he's also
> pussy whipped. His wives won't let him go
> whoring.

screwy

This word would seem to mean someone who likes
to **screw.** It doesn't. It describes a crazy or otherwise
wrong-headed person.

example:

> *Barney:* What's the matter with Louisa? Doesn't
> she like to screw?
>
> *Homer:* Nah. She's screwy.

whoreson dog

Your mother's a **whore,** and you're a dog! A splen-
did curse in print, but when you pronounce it, communication breaks down.

example:

> *Sussex:* You whoreson dog!
>
> *Essex:* Are you calling me a horse and dog?
>
> *Sussex:* Exactly!
>
> *Essex:* You're a weird fuck, Sussex, but for what
> it's worth, I'll play your twisted little
> game—you cow and cat!

Need to Know

cunt struck
eye-opener
pussy whipped

Nice to Know

assholed
charity fuck
mercy fuck

Forget It

beaver cleaver
Honoré Balzac
horse cock
screwy
whoreson dog

∗ ∗ ∗ ∗ ∗ ∗ ∗ ∗ ∗ ∗ ∗ ∗ ∗

Tips

> *Q. What's the biggest drawback in Africa?*
> *A. An elephant's foreskin*
> —EDGAR RICE BURROUGHS

Let's cut to the chase:

hatband

In parts of Texas the **foreskin** is called a **hatband.**
(The Texas-based Dixie Chicks call it an **aardvark.***)

lace curtains

Irish immigrants who became successful in America were called lace-curtain Irish. So what? It has nothing to do with this term for a foreskin.

snapper

This name for the foreskin is also the name for a **cunt.** Confusing, eh?

---

*Do not confuse this with **aardvarking about.** (See **The Gang's All Here** section.)

whickerbill

In Arkansas, **whickerbill** is a common term for the foreskin.

uncut dick

This is the **dick** of an un-circumcised man. Circumcised men who want an **uncut dick** can have a plastic surgeon restore the **foreskin,** leaving them with a **fauxskin.**

example:

Irv: I'm going to Texarkana to get me a new whickerbill.

Sean: Make sure the hatband's not too tight. Doctors are notorious for leaving small tips.

Bitter Butter

❉

In *English as a Second F*cking Language,* we mentioned that none of our Distinguished Panel of Experts had ever personally heard **jizz** referred to as **duck butter.**

Small wonder!

Several thoughtful correspondents noted that **duck butter** is not **jizz** at all. According to one articulate reader, "It's the cheese-like, foul-smelling, sebaceous secretion that can accumulate under a foreskin."

As reasonable men and women, we're willing to accept that definition. Still we're faced with an overwhelming question:

Why isn't the expression **duck butter** more widely used?

Perhaps it's because the technical term for the funky gunk in question is **smegma,** a repulsive word, well suited to its meaning. Quite simply, it doesn't cry out for an equivalent.

That said, we urge all you uncircumsized philistines to peel back your **whickerbills,** wash your **dick heads,** and consider the couplet attributed to the late Dorothy Parker, a longtime writer for the *New Yorker* and one of the fabled "Algonquin Wits":

Is your girlfriend phlegmatic?
Perhaps you're smegmatic.

The Gang's All Here

＊

What should you call those precious intimate moments that involve a **whole fucking bunch** of people?

Joe Bob Briggs, the syndicated drive-in movie critic, refers to sex involving three or more persons as "aardvarking around in weird combinations, making the sign of the triple-snouted octopus."

Here are some brief alternatives:

threesie

This is three people **aardvarking,** etc.

group grope

This sort of get-together is, ideally, a **come-together.**

Mongolian cluster fuck

A **group grope** on a grand scale.

example:

    Floyd: I just heard a Dan Quayle speech. It was really fucking confusing.

    Ruby: I just got back from a Mongolian cluster fuck. It was really confusing fucking.

The term can also describe a disastrous turn of events—a **SNAFU.**

example:

    Earl: Jasmine used the wrong mailing list when she sent out the invitations for the group grope. We got a bunch of philatelists who were more interested in licking stamps than each other.

    Merle: Sounds like a Mongolian cluster fuck to me.

Idioms

*Q: If you call a dog's dick a leg,
how·many legs does a dog have?
A: Four. Don't matter what you call it,
a dog's dick is still his dick.*
—JACK LONDON, *THE CALL OF THE WILD*

bareback

This means not wearing a **rubber** while **fucking.**

example:

Calamity: What brings you to the straddle academy, cowboy?

Clint: I want to get back in the saddle again.

Calamity: Then mount up—so long as you don't ride bareback.

bork

A specialized **fart,** and a superb example of onomatopoeia. If you fart in the bathtub, this is the sound you hear when the bubble reaches the surface and bursts.*

---

*Historical note: In 1987 Robert Bork's nomination to the Supreme Court of the United States was rejected for fear people would refer to him as Justice Bathtubfartbubble, a Germanic-sounding name that could prove distracting to other members of the Court.

cooter

In Maine and neighboring states, a **cooter*** does not correspond to any *specific* part of the human body. Rather, it is a term for any body part the viewer thinks should not be seen.

example:

> *Eugene:* Did Alice show you her box?
> *Craig:* No. Her box turtle. But she wasn't wearing panties, and when she bent over to get it out of its box, I saw her cooter.

fluffer

A stimulating occupation. By hand, mouth, or other means, a fluffer gives **hard-ons** to flagging actors in porn or other films.

example:

> *Kiersten:* That fucking director fired me.
> *Peaches:* Why? Did you fluff your lines?
> *Kiersten:* No. I refused to fluff the leading man.

It's just as well Kiersten was fired. With the rise of Viagra, most fluffers lost their jobs, anyway. A few have found work in the organic porn films sold at health food stores.

---

*Residents of Alabama and Georgia call a box turtle a "cooter." We don't know what their word for **cooter** is—if any.

horse you rode in on

This is a horse of a different color. It is a meta-phorical horse and appears only in the phrase **Fuck you and the horse you rode in on.** It is used when a simple **Fuck you!** is not enough.

example:

> *Mrs. Thatcher:* You're staying after school, young man! Nobody says, "Fuck you!" in my classroom.
>
> *Johnnie:* In that case, fuck you and the horse you rode in on!

How's your hammer hanging?

In this expression, **hammer** is a name for the **prick,** but *only* in this expression. It means "How are you?"

How's your ass?

A Cape Cod pleasantry. It's just a way of saying hello, but it can cause communication problems.

example:

> *Horace:* How's your ass?
>
> *Hortense:* Shut up!
>
> *Horace:* Mine, too. Must be the salt air.

farts still whistle

A term a man just released from incarceration might use. It indicates that his preference for not being **corn-holed** was honored. He has kept a **tight ass-hole.**

flip a bitch

This is neither dog judo nor **giving the finger** to a nasty woman. It means making a U-turn.

example:

    Horst: I heard some guy in a VW flipped a bitch on Hollywood Boulevard and almost creamed your Hummer. Did you terminate him?

    Arnold: No. It was a girl only, so I just flipped the bitch off and kept going.

fucknugget

A clueless person. Not quite an **asshole,** but possibly an **ass clown** or a **numbnuts.**

example:

    Timmy: Hey, did you tell the boss I was an ass clown?

    Jessica: No, numbnuts, I said you were a fucknugget.

gamahuching

This is an elegant term for **eating pussy.** It is best used when entertaining foreign dignitaries or addressing civic organizations. In the ordinary course of business, terms such as **carpet munching, muff diving,** or **pearl diving** will suffice.

gristle whistle, blowing the

This means **giving a blow job.** Although this image is extravagant, our panelists find it agreeable by virtue of its *heft.*

hoover

Contrary to popular belief, this term for **giving a blow job** does not come from a twentieth century U.S. President who **sucked,** but from a vacuum cleaner.

example:

   Engelbert: Did Gretel blow the gristle whistle last night?

   Hansel: I'll say! She hoovered my dick until my head caved in.

one-eyed mother fucker

The **average mother fucker** has two eyes. Oedipus—the **classic mother fucker**—didn't have any. In between the extremes we find the **one-eyed mother fucker,** which is an all-purpose simile. It's often employed in stressful times, when the *mot juste** doesn't leap to mind.

example:

   Jocasta: You little mother fucker, what did you do with my brooch?

   Oedipus: Mother, I cannot tell a lie. I used it to put out my eyes.

   Jocasta: Euh! That must hurt like a one-eyed mother fucker!

   Oedipus: Only when I laugh. By the way, Mom, did you come yet?

---

*French words.

phone sex

If this were a term for using a telephone as a **dildo,** it would be in the **Banned Devices** section. But it isn't. **Phone sex** is the practice of talking with someone on the phone while **jerking off** or **finger fucking** oneself. That's the theory. But unless the parties involved have video phones, neither can know for sure that the other is putting theory into practice. On the upside, phone sex is an effective strategy for birth control and for faking erections.

pitching a tent

This is the term used for erecting a portable shelter, usually of canvas or other waterproof fabric. It also means getting a **hard-on.** The expression comes from the conical bulge in the trousers of **horny** men. Logic suggests we should say **raising a teepee.** But we don't. The fact is, a **hard-on** knows no logic.

example:

Lenny: I think it's time to pitch a tent, hon.

Jolene: Great. But first I think we'd better erect some kind of portable shelter of canvas or other waterproof fabric. I don't like fucking in the rain.

prick with ears

This is not some type of **French tickler** (see **Banned Devices** section), but a mean-spirited man. By adding "with ears" the speaker makes it clear the **prick** in question is a **metaphorical prick,** not the desirable kind.

prick with wheels

This is a British term for a **prick with ears.**

example

Ginnie: Stood up again, eh? Your boyfriend Ian's a prick with ears.

Minnie: I wouldn't say that. Besides, he drives a brand-new Rolls Royce.

Ginnie: Okay. He's a prick with wheels.

pulling the taffy

This is **jerking off** and the **taffy** pulled is a **prick,** but only in this context. The term, which also refers to engaging in trivial or doomed activities, is used at most amusement parks, seaside resorts, and gambling casinos.

example:

Conny: You've been pulling on that slot machine all night. How's it going?

Bill: So-so. I'm down nine-million bucks.

Conny: Might be wiser to stay home and pull your taffy.

Bill: That would be imprudent.

putting the lipstick to the dipstick

This means **giving a blow job.** It is the only time a **prick** should be called a **dipstick.**

example:

Hillie: Did you have sex with that woman?

Willie: Absolutely not. Although she did put the lipstick to the dipstick.

saddle, in the

A Wild West term for **fucking.**

straddle academy

This is an elegant term for a **whorehouse.**

'taint

This is not a Chinese dynasty. It is the **perineum,** the area between a woman's **asshole** and her **cunt.** 'Tain't her asshole and 'taint her cunt; it's her **'taint.**

tangle assholes

If you have a problem visualizing this, don't bother seeing an eye doctor; the image is better imagined than seen. It means getting into a strong disagreement with someone, maybe even coming to blows.

example:

>   *Charlie:*   Hey, asshole!
>   *Orlando:*   Cool it with that asshole stuff. You don't want to tangle assholes with me—asshole!

un-ass

This odd little verb is used exclusively with the word *chair.* It's usually used by someone who's higher up the chain of command than you, whose territory you've invaded. Under no circumstances should you speak of **assing** a chair.

example:

>   *Captain Kirk:*   Un-ass that chair, Scotty, or I'll have your ass!

| Scotty: | Fook!* I nae* can catch a fookin'* break. |

whip it

This means to **jerk off,** the **it** being the **prick,** which is **whipped** into a lather.

whip off

Who'd have guessed? This also means **jerk off.**

whip it out

This means to suddenly expose your **prick,** usually in an erect state.

whipout

This is mad money, ready cash that you can whip out of your pocket for instant gratification.

example:

| Henry: | I heard you whipped it out at Darlene's Diner last night. |
| Lamont: | Yeah. I wanted Darlene to whip me off in the back booth, but when she found out I didn't have any whipout she told me to zip out to my truck and whip it myself. |

wicked fuckin' good

This is high praise in New England and is useful for describing any good thing, from a **free blow job** to a

---

*Scottish dialect.

mocha frappe. The highest praise would be **wicked fuckin' pisser** (pronounced **wickid fuckin' pissah**).

example:

    Dorcas: Was it* good for you?
    Gideon: Wickid fuckin' pissah!

---

*free blow job/mocha frappe

* * * * * * * * * * * * *

Final F*cking Exam

*

It's time to test your swearing skills.

Circle the letter next to the *best* answer to each of the following questions. You have fifteen minutes to complete the exam. If you need more time, take it.

Begin

1. You haven't had a bite to eat for two days, so as soon as you've cashed out your lottery winnings you head for a gourmet restaurant. You decline a menu and say, "Give me two of everything. I'm so hungry I could eat
   a. a large meal."
   b. the Vienna Boys Choir."
   c. the asshole out of a skunk."

2. A good definition of a "stand-up fuck" is
   a. a mobster who won't rat on his pals.
   b. a rude person who doesn't show up for a date.
   c. a knee trembler.

3. A woman who displays a prominent "camel toe" is said to be
   a. yet another tragic victim of Egyptian hoof and mouth disease.
   b. a foot fetishist's dream girl.
   c. hung like a donut.

4. At two o'clock in the morning, you wake with a jolt. Are those footsteps on the stairs? You slide your AK-47 from under the bed and tip-toe out to the hallway. Something moves in the dim light and you let rip with a burst from your weapon. When you flip on the light, you see that you've singed your tabby cat's fur and demolished your giant-screen TV. You go back to bed and your wife asks what the fuss was all about. You say it was no big thing, just
   a. a smoldering pussy.
   b. a hot twat.
   c. cunt smoke.

5. You are an immigrant, hungry, tired and desperate for work. A man in a white suit and expensive Panama hat approaches you. "Welcome to California," he says. "Plenty of work here, if you don't mind breathing pesticides, living in a shack, and working long hours under grueling conditions for less than minimum wage. By the way, got milk?"

You say to him,

a. "No, sir, but some day I hope to have part ownership of a cow."

b. "You are unbearably kind to speak to a humble person like myself."

c. "I shit in the milk of thy whore of a mother."

6. When your heifer backs up to greet your meat, she is
   a. a dumb fuck.
   b. dumbstruck.
   c. stump broke.

7. As Mr. Weems steps up to the post office window to mail a postcard, the clerk puts out a CLOSED sign. "I've decided to knock off early," he says.

   Mr. Weems looks at his watch. It's 10:14 in the morning. He frowns and says, "Oh, fiddlesticks!"

   The clerk gives him a hard look. "You got a problem?"

   Mr. Weems clears his throat. "Oh, no," he says. "That's fine, I can mail this tomorrow. Have a nice day."

   Mr. Weems is obviously

   a. a man with a paisley ascot.
   b. a man with a Warhol pastel.
   c. a man with a paper asshole.

8. After perusing the *Sports Illustrated* swim-suit issue for a half hour, George glances down at the bulge in his pants and realizes he is
   a. as corny as Kansas in August.
   b. as ornery as a piebald bandicoot.
   c. as horny as a three-balled billy goat.

9. A fluffer

    a. arranges your hotel pillow.

    b. makes a lot of mistakes.

    c. makes it hard for actors.

10. A man is on a New Age retreat when an attractive
    woman in his group suggests they fuck. It's a scin-
    tillating prospect, but he thinks of his wife and the
    little ones at home. He tells the woman her sug-
    gestion is out of the question at that time and asks
    her to

    a. try to act more mystic.

    b. give him a raincheck.

    c. put the lipstick to the dipstick.

Scoring is as follows:

> 0 points for every *a.* answer;
>
> 0 points for every *b.* answer;
>
> 10 points for every *c.* answer

You must score 100 points to pass the exam. If you
don't pass the exam, take it again. Continue taking it
until you do pass.

Remember: if a fucking thing's worth doing, it's
worth doing fucking well.

✻ ✻ ✻ ✻ ✻ ✻ ✻ ✻ ✻ ✻ ✻ ✻

SHAWN MEHRA

World renowned for his innovative lectures and workshops, **Professor Sterling Johnson** has been teaching English as a second language for over twenty years. He now lives in Pacific Grove, California, where he enjoys a "nice f*cking day" as much as the next fellow.

Want to join my distinguished panel of experts? If you'd like to see your favorite swear or expression in print, send it to Sterling Johnson, St. Martin's Press, Suite 1700, 175 Fifth Avenue, New York, N.Y. 10010.

You can also e-mail entries to rokaco@redshift.com.

I'm sorry that no credit or compensation can be given, but I love hearing from readers who share my passion for language!